San Francisco's Heritage in Art Glass

San Francisco's Heritage in Art Glass

By Edith Hopps Powell
Photography - Brian Moran

SALISBURY PRESS
SUPERIOR PUBLISHING COMPANY
SEATTLE

Library of Congress Cataloging in Publication Data

Powell, Edith H.
San Francisco's heritage in art glass.

1. United Art Glass Company.
2. Glassware — California — San Francisco.
3. Decoration and ornament — Art nouveau.
I. Moran, Brian.
II. Title.
NK5112.P68 748.2'9194'61 76-2527
ISBN 0-87564-013-3

FIRST EDITION

CONTENTS

DEDICATION

TO MY HUSBAND AND FOR OUR GIRLS.
MAY THEY CHERISH ALWAYS THEIR
INHERITED LOVE OF BEAUTY.

SAN FRANCISCO

The city that rose from the ashes,
So proudly you stand by the Bay
Lose not the spirit that made you
The city that you are today.

Treasure your long-time traditions
Born of great joy and deep sorrow
Cherish the past and its beauty
Keep it today for tomorrow.

FOREWORD

Represented in this book are art glass windows and domes produced by The United Glass Co., which flourished in San Francisco between the years 1895 and 1915, under the aegeas of the brothers Harry and Bert Hopps, who were the owners and designers for the company. The quality of the work produced by the organization was a reflection of their heritage. They were grandsons of Charles Hopps of the well-known firm of Hopps & Sons, established in 1850. Speaking of that firm, from the archives of the California Historical Society comes the quotation — "excels in their business, displaying exceptional skill and ability in their manner of executing work, while the result is of such a nature as to please the most critical".

When discussing art glass, as distinguished from stained glass, which is primarily translucent, one refers to a glass that is more opaque, iridescent and reflective, but very effective in its own right. These particular properties required their own special handling to achieve the optimum potential of the glass and this found its fullest flowering in the Art Nouveau mode which originated in Germany and was the preponderant art glass style between 1895 and 1910.

The onset of World War I brought the end of the functioning of The United Glass Co., which depended on both England and Germany for many of its glasses. It also marked the termination of the Art Nouveau period. Its recent revival, in the 1960's, has stimulated a special interest in Tiffany glass and other art glass creations of the period.

Art glass is considered a unique American development in contrast to stained glass with its Byzantine and Medieval origins. Although opaque glass had been produced in Europe and America during the early nineteenth century, it was merely used for containers for household use. It was the experiments of John La Farge and Louis Tiffany, beginning in the late 1870's, that really created the particular glasses that became known as art glass, specifically for picture windows and domes. Both men traveled and studied art in Europe, were artistic by nature, and brought their abilities to bear in creating new types of effects with glass. They experimented separately, but with equal interest to introduce color to glass in unique ways heretofore unknown. John La Farge was credited with developing Amerina and Burmese glass. Louis Tiffany created Faurille glass, which included gold lustre, Mazarin Blue, Tel el Avano and aquamarine.

Often called the opalescent style, this well describes the art glass genre. To further clarify the term art glass, it is found that superior works include antique glass, semi-opaque glass, painted glass, glass jewels and perhaps bottle bottoms, actually called rondelles, in various combinations. This experimentation with new types of glass was to expand the possibilities for different effects and to somewhat lighten the palette from the deep colors of traditional stained glass to the more golden sunlight tones.

In fact the possibilities were not unlimited, but consolidated into a quite recognizable opulent style. Unfortunate to relate is the fact that really inferior works of poor glass and canned or catalogue designs also proliferated during the period and contributed to a general degeneration of the art glass mode. This eventually led to art glass being dismissed as an art form in the post World War I period and the revival of the traditional stained glass media and methods. Cubistic abstraction and abstract expressionism were easily adapted to the older tradition, whereas the stylization and realism of Art Nouveau were more suited to art glass.

PROLOGUE

ne of the earliest memories of my childhood was to visit the United Art Glass Co., owned by my family. The large tables with the colored glass, cut in every imaginable shape and fitted like a jigsaw puzzle, the glaziers with the soldering irons working to join the lead, zinc or copper (which surrounded each piece of glass), made an indelible impression on a pre-school child. I walked up and down aisles of large pieces of glass, segregated by texture and color, and fitted into sections as neat as a bookshelf. My father and my uncle made designs in black and white on the drawing boards and then beautiful finished paintings in color for the men to copy in glass. If I was a ''good girl'', and did not bother the workers, by staying out of the way of the men cutting glass and the soldering irons, I was allowed to sit like a little princess with a treasure box of jewels and select one of each of them to take home. There were little wooden cigar boxes filled with rubies, amethysts, emeralds, topaz and sapphires. I enjoyed running my fingers through these treasures, then selecting one of each — of beautiful color and beautiful shape. These bits of glass were as precious to me as any crown jewels from royalty and I am positive that they gave me more pleasure than real jewels did to the crowned heads of Europe.

I remember my uncle, in a basso-profundo voice, bellowing forth from his private office ''The Star Spangled Banner'', which was a signal for everyone to stop whatever he was doing and to stand at attention with hand over heart. Then my father would raise a miniature American flag on an 18-inch flagpole — that was done everytime a new contract was closed.

All of the historical art glass in San Francisco done by the United Art Glass Co. was conceived to the national anthem and created in an atmosphere of brotherhood. I learned many years later that the men, belonging to a union, had to go out on strike — but were very upset as they had to strike for less wages than they were receiving from the United Art Glass Co.

The only living survivor of that firm is Otto Dressler, who was a young apprentice in 1909, having just arrived from Germany. He worked on the original dome of the City of Paris in that year, and in 1972 helped to restore the dome for Liberty House. The night the original twelve men completed the installation of the dome, our family gave them a champagne French dinner (appropriate?). When the restoration was complete in 1972, Liberty House gave a champagne party for the twelve men who had done the work, not knowing of the first party. Mr. Dressler has come full circle, from 18 years to 82 years, and is today living among his glorious glass.

Cypress Lawn Cemetery

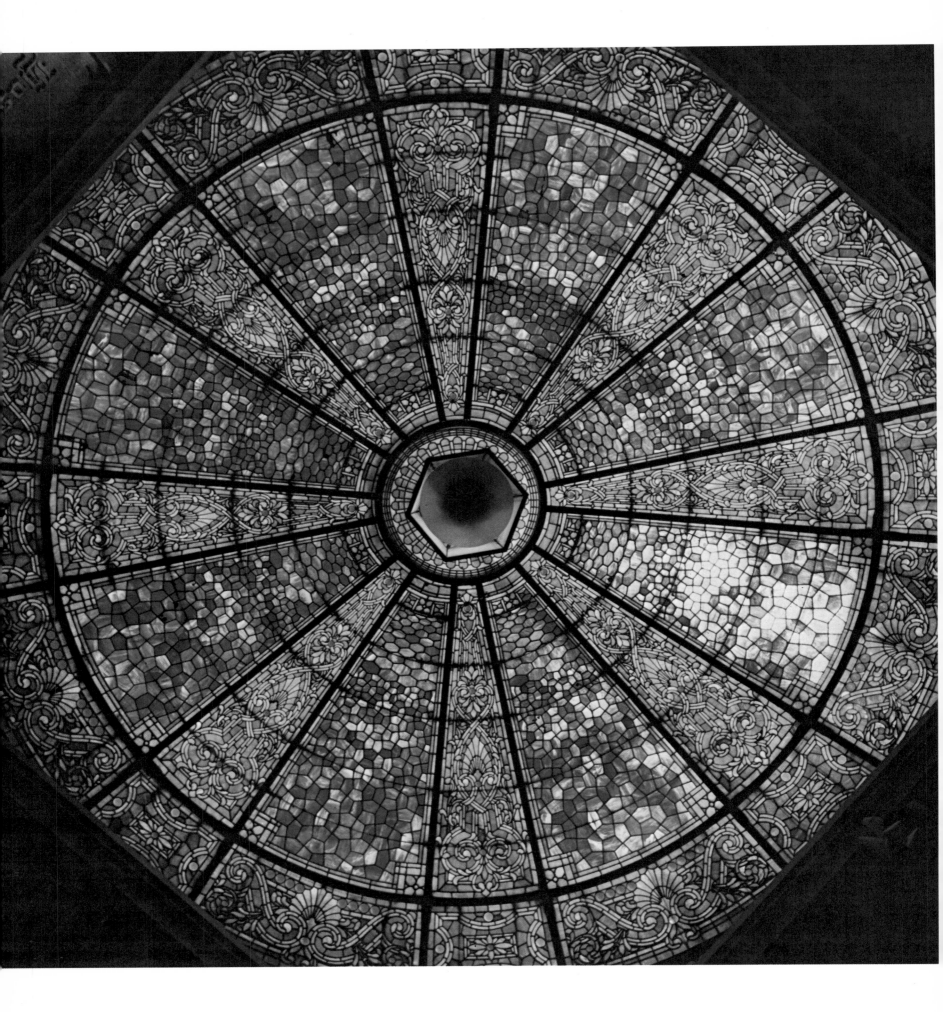

Dramatic Blue and Gold Dome
20′ × 20′

Detail Showing Intricate Design—
A Glass Kaleidoscope of Various Patterns.

Detail Showing Intricate Design of
Multi-Shaped Glass

Small Room—Whole Ceiling Dome—of Red, Green, Blue

Side Glass Framing Dome

60' Ceiling—Crypts on Sides
Interesting Design—Alternating Sections

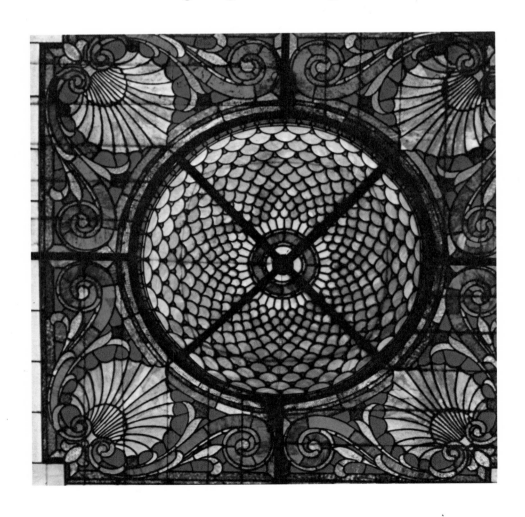

Detail

Ceiling Detail—Shaded Colored Glass

CYPRESS LAWN

t was not a pleasant trip for me (although my mother thought that it was) to go with her to the cemetery on Easter, Christmas, Memorial Day and Anniversaries. It was a very long and tiresome street car ride from the Park-Presidio district to Colma, with all the transfers in between. The final group of people on the last street car were solemn and sad with their arms full of flowers, all going to decorate the graves of their families. It was a long, long walk from the end of the line, up through the "paths of peace", lined with marble angels, and weeping willows. My mother pointed out the resting places of all of our relatives, and especially sad were those of the children that had died so young. I liked it when their toys were put behind glass in the little marble headstones. It was beautiful to see the entire cemetery decorated and to feel that your family never forgot you even when you were dead. Yet, it was more beautiful when we reached the warmth of home with a fire burning, dinner ready and my mother's tears wiped away. Why did it always rain when we went to the cemetery?

WHERE NATURE IS REBORN EACH DAY THEY SLEEP—AND HAVE NOT GONE AWAY

f the cemeteries in South San Francisco, Cypress Lawn is one of the oldest. It was founded through the efforts of H. H. Noble in 1892. Situated on both sides of El Camino Real, with rolling lawns, ponds, weeping willows and cypress trees, a feeling of beauty and serenity encompasses its many acres.

Art glass created early in this century still remains in the original mausoleum, reflecting jewel-like colors in various designs in the rectangular ceilings and small domes.

In this beautiful memorial park are many vaults bearing the names of those that built and made San Francisco famous.

How fitting that their eternal sleep should be so near the city that they loved.

Ceiling Detail—Shaded Colored Glass

Intricate Design of Center of Dome

Bardelli's

Bardelli's Peacock Window

Day or Night Window Enhances Dining Room

BARDELLI'S

When out-of-town visitors say "We would like to have dinner in one of your old and typical San Francisco restaurants" — that means to the San Francisco host a very special place. It means no chrome nor plastic flowers — no bare tables with sawdust on the floors — not a restaurant on the 30th floor with a view of the city and the elegance of Europe's finest. It means an Italian or French restaurant; one that emerged after the earthquake, white damask table cloths and large napkins; a bud vase with fresh flowers on each table in the daytime; and a small lamp or candle replacing it at night, booths in the back where young lovers can have privacy with no eyes for anyone else and no envious eyes on them; with a bell on the wall that calls for the waiter and only then is the curtain drawn aside and the order taken.

The ancestry of Bardelli's begins as an oyster house in 1906 and then in 1911 as Charles Fashion Grill until the owner died in 1946. In 1947 Charles Bardelli, with a fine reputation as chef from Italy to New York to San Francisco, opened the present Bardelli's. His reputation and the perfect food have continued through the years. The historic past is still maintained in the decor, crystal chandeliers, the famous Peacock Window, and other art glass throughout, soft rugs and that indefinable feeling that gives it the San Francisco flavor.

Mr. and Mrs. Stuart Adams are the present owners. Mrs. Adams is the last of the Bardelli family. Her father was the well known Charles Bardelli. As a little girl, she often dined at Charles Fashion Grill, never dreaming that one day she would be the owner of this restaurant.

Bardelli Exterior

As a teen-ager, I was included sometimes with the adults of the family for dinner at Charles Fashion. It was a typical San Francisco restaurant, white linen, carpeted floors, men waiters and substantial food. I enjoyed it, except when there was a mention of the Peacock Window. I felt it was very old fashioned and out of date and hoped they would never mention that "we made that window" if I had a friend with me. As a young lady in my teens, I had "out-grown" San Francisco's art glass and Victorian houses. I was the new generation!

Dome Above Foyer and Peacock Window

Small Windows of Foyer
Continuation of Flowers-Leaves

Silhouette of Peacock at Fountain

Flower Design in Glass Garden—
Effect to Peacock Detail

Water-Design in Mottled Colorless Glass

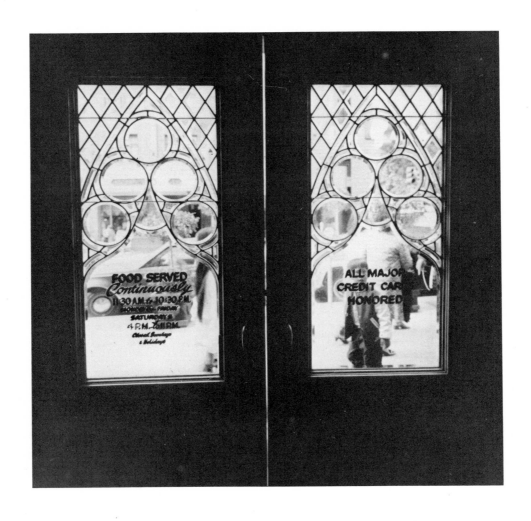

Plate Glass Doors

City of Paris

Elaborate Framework of Dome

Warm Yellow Tones Give
Sunshine Light to Entire Rotunda

The Glass Ship
Replica of Sailing Vessels with Goods from
The Old World

CITY OF PARIS

The "City of Paris", (recently operated by Liberty House,) now in the "National Register", is another landmark of San Francisco. The prestigious firm of Nieman-Marcus of Dallas has plans for replacing the old building with a new six million dollar structure. Mr. Marcus has promised and pledged that the art glass dome would be carefully taken down and recreated in the new store as part of San Francisco's heritage.

For years the oval dome has been a halo of sunlight, shining down on the rotunda and the floors that circle it with their balustrades. Many generations of San Franciscans and their children have gone from floor to floor to look down, but mostly to look up and be closer to the dome, with its beautiful design of a ship — significant of the treasures brought from France. Christmas was not Christmas in San Francisco unless it included a good long look at the mammoth Christmas tree that stood in the rotunda and reached to the sky. As we looked up at the gorgeous tree, we saw childrens' faces peering over the balustrades, like angels from old world paintings. The "City of Paris" tree was the dream of every child — a tree so big that tricycles and doll buggies, skates and skis were the ornaments! The huge silver star on the top shimmered against the background of the golden dome — "our dome", as my mother always told us. Strange that it was "our dome", or was it Fate? My father, an art student, was talented and possessed a marvelous eye for color. His first opportunity and job was working with beautiful fabrics imported by the "City of Paris". At that time tapestries and silks were used as wall coverings. My grandfather had obtained this position for him through a personal friend and was anxious that my father utilize every minute and learn all that he could. One day this self-confident young man extended his lunch hour through the entire afternoon. When he returned to work, he thought it best to resign, rather than be fired, which was done in those days. My grandfather was so furious with his young son, and so embarrassed at the ingratitude of the boy, that his punishment was a menial job as an apprentice in the family firm. Eventually, time has a way, — he was back working at the "City of Paris", constructing the dome, done by the United Glass Co. in 1909.

What could be more fun for a little girl than to go down town on Saturday afternoon? I wore my black patent leather shoes, with gray cloth tops with laces above my ankles, long white stockings, a French blue broadcloth coat (from Schonwasser's), hair in braids, and always white gloves. No well-dressed San Francisco child from two years of age on ever appeared downtown without gloves. When we shopped at the City of Paris, I felt very important, as I looked at the big dome and knew where it has been made and how it had been made, and secretly felt it was "ours". The White House on Saturdays gave away huge white balloons on a stick, but I liked the balloon man better. He stood in front of the City of Paris with a wonderful bouquet of balloons, and I could choose one to take home. After shopping, my mother would let us follow the strains of music from the organ grinder, so that I could see the monkey perform, and then with his tiny hands, pick up the coins I tossed him (he always put one in his mouth and bit it to see if it was good). How strange that every Saturday was a sunny day in downtown San Francisco.

Dome from Top Floor

Interesting Detail of Top Floor

San Francisco Christmas Tradition
"The City of Paris Christmas Tree"
Crowned by Art Glass Dome of Rotunda

Beautiful Rotunda Encircles
Christmas Tree

Old Cornerstone and Famous Corner
Geary and Stockton Streets with Typical
San Francisco Flower Stand

Palace Hotel

Palace Court—Historic Room

THE PALACE HOTEL

The Garden Court of the Sheraton Palace Hotel, called "the most beautiful dining room in the world" by world famous personalities, as well as San Franciscans, was once an open sun-court. It was filled with flowers and greenery and was the carriage entrance to the hotel. Imagine the experience of driving through a garden to a metropolitan hotel!

The fire of 1906 destroyed the famed luxury hotel, built in 1874. When it was rebuilt, the grand court (110 by 85 feet wide) was covered by a dome of iridescent glass. The United Glass Co. made a splendid arch of glass, giving the dining room an amber reflection from the sunlight. The dome is 48 feet high and adds to the spectacular beauty of this room, circled by Ionic columns of Italian marble, huge crystal chandeliers, velvet hangings and mirrored doors.

International personalities and great world figures have attended historical and social events in this room. Long remembered was the League of Nations speech made here in 1919 by President Woodrow Wilson. Names such as Winston Churchill, Nixon, Eisenhower, John and Robert Kennedy, Madame Chiang Kai-shek, Thomas Edison, Queen Juliana, Nikita Kruschev, Rockefeller, Konrad Adenauer, Franklin Roosevelt, all have enjoyed San Francisco hospitality in this room. If one has not dined here, one has missed a San Francisco experience. Its history, present and past, is the reason that the Garden Court has been declared officially a San Francisco landmark.

PALACE COURT

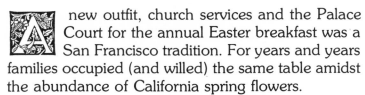A new outfit, church services and the Palace Court for the annual Easter breakfast was a San Francisco tradition. For years and years families occupied (and willed) the same table amidst the abundance of California spring flowers.

There was an elegance about it never to be forgotten; the setting, soft music and delicious food. What child could ever forget the spun sugar in the shape of a bird's nest, with tiny colored eggs, the huge pink velvet bunnies and those fantastic Easter baskets?

This Room Measures 110′ × 85′
Ionic Columns and Chandeliers Give a Classic Beauty

Luncheon Dining in Court—A Tradition
in San Francisco

Entrance of Palace Hotel

Hibernia Bank

Dome of Hibernia Bank with Elaborate Frame Design

Circular Dome is Smaller Complement
to Oblong Large Dome

Oblong Dome—Approximately 25′ × 60′

Interesting Design—
Showing Support Arches

HIBERNIA BANK

In 1899 my mother and father were married. One of the first duties of young couples at that time was to open a bank account. When my mother filled out an application, the teller asked "What is your husband's first name?". "Bert", she answered. "Young lady, Bert is not a name; is it Albert, Robert, Herbert?" "It is just Bert, she said. His patience at an end, he tore up the application slowly and deliberately, and said in a velvety Irish brogue, "Go home and find out whom you married". With all the dignity of a twenty-year-old, she haughtily flounced out of the bank. She told my father tearfully that night "I will never go in the Hibernia Bank again". But she did, years later, and proudly, as she and "Bert" admired the golden domes that my father and his firm created.

arades were exciting events in my childhood. People in costumes, bands playing, flags flying and to me everyone in the whole world standing along the curbs of Market Street. As a yound child and to this day I feel embarrassed watching a parade. I feel embarrassed for the people in it. Why? Maybe the experience of my parents laughing when "The Hibernians", in green uniforms, passed and I asked "Are they all from the bank?"

Lace Effect of Round Dome

Pinwheel Effect of Round Dome

Skylight in Hibernia Bank

Early 1900's
"Under Clock" Meeting Place

HIBERNIA BANK

he Hibernia Bank represents the strength of Gibraltar — and everlasting as the hills — it never takes chances."

This quotation, from a San Francisco news letter of 1905, is more timely today than when it was written. With the "strength of Gibraltar", it rose from the ashes of the earthquake and fire of 1906. Some of the iron work of the beautiful round and rectangular domes survived the fire. They were replaced with the glass that can be seen today, reflecting a warm and sunny glow to the main floor of the bank at all times.

Over a hundred years old, The Hibernia Bank has lived up to its reputation as being "everlasting as the hills". It was born in the early history of San Francisco and will live on in the future of this great city.

City Hall

Exterior of San Francisco's Handsome
City Hall

Window Detail of Architecture

Ornate Decoration—End of Lobby

Interesting Varied Designs
of Interior of Rotunda

Simple Windows of Colorless Glass
Afford Dignified Feeling

CITY HALL

he impressive City Hall was my introduction to "government". I remember standing in that huge rotunda, looking up to the dome and pretending I was in the Capitol at Washington, D.C. If only the President of the United States would come down that marble stairway, I could greet him and tell him I was from California. The reverie was over when my father took my hand and said "We can go home now, the taxes are paid".

Arch-Shaped Windows
Add Continuity to Rounded Domes of Ceiling
and Curves of Side Ceiling

SAN FRANCISCO CITY HALL

he handsome City Hall of San Francisco is considered one of the most beautiful municipal type buildings in our country. It is the most distinctive building of the civic center complex and one of the finest designs of the architects, Bakewell and Brown. Covering two city blocks, it contains the Mayor's office, administrative offices for the supervisors, courts and various other city departments.

The present City Hall was born after the calamity of 1906 which destroyed the previous one. How fortunate for San Francisco that the wise city fathers of that terrible period took time to plan the reconstruction, not only of a city hall but a civic center. It took them several years to arrive at an agreement. The decision was expedited by the projected plans of the Panama Pacific Exposition for 1915. Could San Francisco consider entertaining distinguished people from all over the world without buildings in which to greet them? The incentive was there, the time was right, it was the opportune moment to have complete cooperation. The city planners, the architects, the citizens, enthusiastically supported the idea of a great civic center. It would be an asset for the future, as well as providing needed facilities for the great new San Francisco rising majestically out of destruction.

Advice and suggestions for plans came from the finest architects, John Galen Howard, Willis Polk and E. H. Bennett. The stunning plan for the civic center were created by John Galen Howard, John Reed Jr. and Fred H. Meyer.

Unlike the other buildings of the complex, the city hall's outstanding feature is a dome, 300 feet above ground level. The architecture possesses great dignity and authority, very European in feeling. The intricate and elaborate gilded ironwork gives an unrivaled decorative facade to the public building.

It is interesting to compare the use and integration of colorless leaded glass windows into the graceful arches of the window areas, instead of a slightly tinted shade of amber, which was so prevalent at the time. Today, this building is as attractive as when it was built.

The interior stairways of marble, the huge rotunda with the light streaming through the leaded glass windows, does credit to those early architects who dreamed of a city hall worthy of the rapidly growing and beautiful city of San Francisco.

Olympic Club

Ceiling of Swimming Pool

One of Several Domes of Olympic Club

OLYMPIC CLUB

here was an aura around the words "Olympic Club". I did not know what it was or where it was, but it was important! There was lots of laughing and happy talk when my mother played the piano for my young uncle to rehearse singing new songs for the minstrel show (whatever that was). Though it was past my bedtime, I would sit on the stairs peeking through the bannisters to listen to their music and wonder why he sang the words in such a funny way.

Art Glass Gives Sun and Warmth
to Pool Below
Artificial Outdoor Daylight
for the Swimmers

OLYMPIC CLUB

he Olympic Club on Post Street is the grandchild of the California Olympic Club of the 1860's, where the young men of that period learned club swinging, boxing, tumbling, vaulting, fencing and other acrobatic feats. The old building on New Montgomery and Howard Sts. had a grand opening ball on January 19th, 1872. It was a night to remember, as it was the climax of years of dedication on the part of its members. For "the benefit of the building fund" there had been numerous programs, plays, minstrel shows, until the participants were quite exhausted. Yet all were able to enjoy and celebrate the Grand Ball.

After the San Francisco devastation of 1906 another Olympic Club was built with the same enthusiasm of the members as their fathers showed in 1871. The handsome club on Post Street, with its art glass of the period, was considered a great addition to San Francisco's restoration. All that remains today of the decorative glass in the club is the skylight and dome over the swimming pool. The panels of glass depicting scenes of Indians have gone in the intervening years of redecorating.

The Olympic Club of the 1970's is as popular as the one of the 1870's. With a heritage of over a hundred years, the club roster can be proud and boast of families encompassing several generations. Much of San Francisco's history is interwoven with the long line of distinguished citizens that have been members of the Olympic Club.

Woodside Home

California Coast in Art Glass

coloring book was my introduction to art. How I treasured my box of crayons with their bright vivid colors! How I enjoyed selecting the outlined designs for my pictures! It was so difficult to keep my hand steady and not go outside of the line when I was coloring. If I made a mistake, or did not like my choice of colors, I turned the page and began another "masterpiece", but I never gave up! It was fun and I enjoyed thinking I was making art glass windows. Jig-saw puzzles have many colors, so would my pictures, just as the art glass in our home. No one ever laughed at my efforts nor discouraged me. Imagine the contrast, a child's crude "kaleidoscope" pictures hung on the wall of a room with a scenic art glass window? "Home is where the heart is" must have been my mothers daily thought as she tolerated my art work — or did she feel that I would see the difference and hopefully develop good taste in art?

Color Tones Change with Sunshine and Shadows

Art Glass or is it Clear Glass with a View?

SCENIC WINDOW

One of the most impressive windows in art glass was done in 1911. It depicts a true California scene, one of the many picturesque spots on the coast. Typical of Carmel and the Monterey area are the ever-blue Pacific, wind swept cypress trees, seal rocks, and the changing colors of the sky. To capture this in glass reflects an imaginative artist, who brought the beauty of the coast to an inland home.

Originally designed and executed in San Francisco, it was, for many years, in a San Mateo residence. When that home was demolished, it was saved. Restored with a framework of rondelles, it is now a dramatic part of a beautiful home in Woodside. It has been so well placed architecturally that it can be enjoyed from the outside as well as the inside. During the day, natural light on both sides of the glass show this scenic window in its true colors. At night, artificial light makes it a very decorative part of the home.

Nautical Window

Early Days on San Francisco Bay

Pale But Pleasing Colors of Sky and Water

One high-light of going to The United Glass Co. was the treat we would have before we started home on the streetcar. There was an ice cream parlor nearby with small round wire-type tables and chairs. Scenes were painted on the walls of dancing girls with ruffled skirts, large floppy hats and high-buttoned shoes. Most important of all, there was a delicious aroma of vanilla. In my most grown-up way, I would order a "Flora-Dora" — vanilla ice cream. It had the most marvelous taste — never to be recaptured in any dessert for the rest of my life.

When we finished our treat, I could then select some candy from the glass cases. The bon-bons and chocolate creams were too grownup for me. I liked the penny candy case, with its variety, all colors, all shapes, all flavors and miniature everything — from trains to animals. Imagine the difficulty in making the momentous decision of what to choose? Two marshmallows for one cent, a licorice whip, a ribbon of paper with colored sugar drops on it and a tiny baby bottle filled with sugar pills, all for five cents. What a happy ending to the day!

Early San Francisco Building

NAUTICAL WINDOW

n Golden Gate Avenue, the street to the rear of the old United Glass Co., stands an early day Knights of Columbus building with an arch of art glass over the entrance to the lobby. The design added a bit of interest to the unimaginative architecture of the foyer. There have been several owners of the building since it was constructed, but the glass remains. After sixty five years, the ship design, so often used by my father, is well defined in lead and in perfect condition. The original slight color of the glass is visible in the sunlight.

The Corinthian Yacht Club was a great influencing force in promoting the love of boating for early San Franciscans. Small sailboats on the Bay was a theme for California artists, whether the medium was watercolor or oil, and many became famous for them.

At The California Historical Society, one finds chapter headings, book-plates and cover designs showing a hallmark of San Francisco, that is, a silhouette of the Golden Gate with sailboats in the foreground.

With the popularity of water sports increasing, San Francisco Bay appears often to be covered with white-winged birds as the sunlight is reflected on the white sails of the yachts. No wonder the Syufy Co. modernized this building but kept the old art glass with the boats for those inside and outside to enjoy.

Victorian House

Victorian House
California and Franklin Streets

VICTORIAN HOUSES

 think I am the only native San Franciscan who hates Victorian houses. Even though I never lived in one, as a child, I thought they looked like the drawings in a coloring-book.

In some areas of the city, there are entire blocks of identical houses lined up straight and prim as Victorian school teachers. Then, of course, there are the many storied mansions with surrounding gardens with aviaries and gazebos and ornate wrought iron fences enclosing the property.

One of these I remember well, as it made an indelible impression on a young child. When we were guests, I was taken with the children to the "play room", which was the entire top floor. It was a child's Christmas Dream. There were life-size vividly painted rocking-horses; miniature over-stuffed furniture, a sofa and arm chairs in ruby red velvet (all of a

size to fit children), tea sets in china cabinets, dolls and animals of all varieties. Most of all, I loved sitting in the little musical rocking-chairs that played a lullabye as I rocked a doll to sleep. That was one Victorian house I could appreciate!

Unlike this story-book playroom for the children was the elegant formal drawing room for the grownups. How sad for them to sit in stiff satin covered chairs not able to look out of those too tall narrow windows with lace curtains and shades drawn. No sunlight ever entered the room, it was cold and austere. I liked our living room where I could cuddle up in the big overstuffed Turkish chair and read a book, or fall asleep in the comfort and security of those happy grown-up voices getting softer and softer.

Art Nouveau Window on Staircase

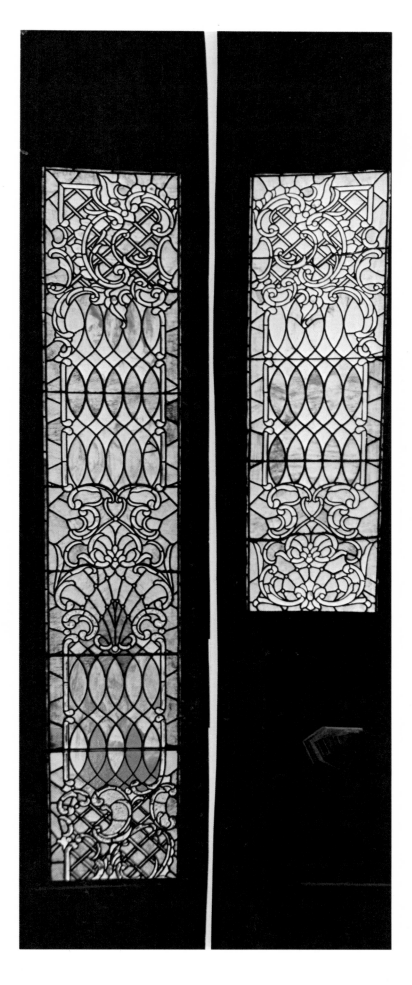

Reception Hall Windows

Victorian House — Designer of Art Glass Unknown

VICTORIAN

here is a movement in San Francisco to restore Victorian houses and put them to good use whether for homes, apartments or for offices. This beautiful example, on the corner of California and Franklin Streets, an historical landmark, is in the process of redecoration. It was the Coleman home in the early 1900's and is now owned by lawyers, Kutsko, Moran & Mullen. Original hand carved woodwork, fireplaces and chandeliers have all been restored for the eleven law offices that surround the staircase and halls.

The light diffused by an elegant art glass window adds warmth and charm to the gracious reception hall that welcomes visitors in the style of early San Francisco.

Stanford Court Hotel

Dome of Closed Court
Stanford Court Hotel

Corner of Historic Site
Powell and California Streets

STANFORD COURT

My mother believed that all children should begin school at the age of seven — especially her children. The child could grow physically playing in the sunshine at the park and the fresh salt air of the ocean beach. The child could grow mentally, maturing in the atmosphere of intelligent parents. I grew! While waiting for the magical first day of school, I learned self-control and patience. My grandmother took me to call on elderly relatives, where I was expected to behave "like a little lady". I was dressed for the occasion in an afternoon dress, long stockings, tailored coat, hat, gloves and purse (play clothes were for one's own garden, casual clothes, as sweaters, for park or beach). One of these elderly cousins lived at the Stanford Court Apartments. I liked to call on her as I could watch the cable cars from the windows while waiting for "tea" to be served with those strange tasting anise cookies.

I enjoyed the varied rhythms made by the clang-clang of the cable car bells. Each grip-man had his own special tune. The happy sounds were constant as the Stanford Court is at the corner of California and Powell Streets, where cable cars cross in all directions.

I learned to read before going to school, but I never dreamed that "Powell", the sign on that corner, would be my married name and that I would read and write it more than any other word in my entire life.

Exterior of Stanford Court Hotel

Art Glass — Stanford Court Hotel — By The Judson
Co. Los Angeles

STANFORD COURT HOTEL

eland Stanford's original mansion was on the site of the present Stanford Court Hotel on Nob Hill. Replacing the private home, destroyed in the fire of 1906, was the Stanford Court Apartments, of impeccable and substantial reputation. In the center of social life on Nob Hill and amidst the gaity of the Hotel Mark Hopkins, Fairmont Hotel and the prestigious Pacific Union Club, these apartments, built at the turn of the century, enjoyed the pageantry of San Francisco's colorful history. Modern conveniences of the present day took precedence over the fading glamour of the early Californians, and so today, we have the elegant Stanford Court Hotel, built within the walls of the Stanford Court Apartments and retaining the handsome exterior architecture of that period.

The Tiffany style art glass dome in the courtyard is a modern example of an old craft and brings to San Francisco the revival of the beauty that enhanced the buildings of the Golden Era.

Mr. Otto Dressler

Mr. Dressler in Workshop of His Retirement

Plate Glass on Work Table
Tiffany Lamps in Background

Designs for Art Glass

MAKING ART GLASS

Original ideas or art work of other artists often suggest designs to the creator of a specific assignment. Sometimes there is a natural theme to be used, such as a replica of the head of Bacchus The God of Wine, with a grape motif surrounding it — for a winery. After completing the design, the artists color it to show exactly how it should appear in glass. This is the guide for the glass cutter in his choice of colors.

A special scissors for cutting up the finished design is used. They are made with a groove in the blade which makes a margin or allowance for the lead (or whatever material is used) to bind the pieces of glass together. The "cartoon" or design is cut into a jigsaw of colors, used for the pattern to be duplicated in glass.

When all of the glass has been cut exactly, as to shape and color, it is ready to be glazed together. The cartoon is placed on a large table and the glass put into the various positions, having been bound with grooved lead. The glazier solders the lead together. Cement is then pressed beneath the flanges to waterproof and make it secure. The reverse is done in the same manner. Support bars are used for large areas, such as domes, skylights or windows.

Mr. Otto Dressler, now eighty two years of age, is the last member of the staff of The United Glass Co. He still restores glass in some of early San Francisco's well-known buildings. His stocks of glass, now over fifty years old, include some of the original inventory of The United Glass Co.

On his various trips to the European centers of glass making, he has obtained an interesting and valuable collection of stained glass. The restoration of the dome of Liberty House (City of Paris) would not have been possible without the cooperation of this last remaining artisan in art glass in San Francisco. The perfection of the dome in its restoration is a tribute to the skill, knowledge and experience of a man whose entire life was devoted to working in glass.

George Hopps Father of Harry and Bert Hopps and Edith Powells' Grandfather Son of Charles Hopps, The Founder of Hopps & Sons Established in 1850.

Cutting Glass

Breaking Excess Glass
Away from Designs

Soldering Rondelles Together

Reinforcing Where Rondelles Join

Finishing Large Design

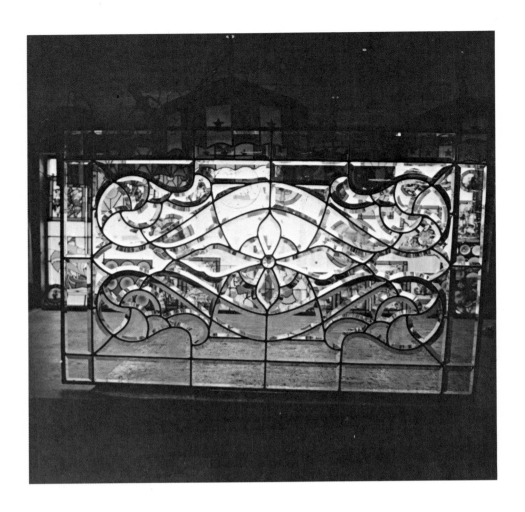

Plate Glass
Gives off Rainbow Lights

Plate Glass Detail

Plate Glass
Finished Window for Door

Adam and Eve
10″ × 15″ Insert for Large Window

Old picture of The United Glass Company plant in San Francisco, must be about 1912. In the right foreground is the young Mr. Dressler, to the rear is Mr. Harry Hopps in the straw hat.

From Mr. Dressler's Collection of Stained Glass and His Own Designs.

From Franz Mayer Co. (1848) Munich, Germany.
Part of Mr. Dressler's European Collection

Rondelle in Center of Geometric Design

Art Glass Rondelles
for Windows or Door Glass

Rondelle in Center of Hexagon
for Large Window

THE CHILD IN A GLASS HOUSE

I lived in a glass house! Not inside of a glass square, nor an ice cube, but in a house that had art glass, beveled glass and stained glass.

When I was a child and opened our beveled glass front door, there I was in the reception hall in the center of a rainbow. Not the usual rainbow, but one broken into a thousand pieces by the sun shining through the bevels or prisms. The colors sparkled and danced as I did, pretending to be a ballerina in a multi-colored spotlight of a stage. At night, it was elegant but only a dignified crystal door.

My mother was the originator of togetherness. After dinner, the family gathered around the cleared off dining table and, instead of games, or jigsaw puzzles, we put copper foil around the edge of little squares of buff-colored glass. We did hundreds of these, one-inch squares that my father took to the United Glass Co. One magical night, when we dashed into dinner, there above the dining room table was a handsome Greek design chandelier that we children had made! (or thought we did).

Whenever I took my little friends upstairs, they made me stop on each landing and explain the "Pictures of stained glass" in the centers of the leaded glass windows. They were the family crest and, of course, the oak tree meant strength, the shells romance, the hand extended for friendship and willingness to help. This was significant as it was family heritage, past, present and future.

One part of our house was really a glass house — the sunporch. It had an art glass roof of orange and yellow nasturtiums trailing like vines over the pale green glass. The wooden railing of the porch was hidden on the inside by mottled opaque green glass beneath clear glass windows above. The creek that ran through the garden near the overhanging sunporch, gave a sound of coolness in summer. In winter, no matter how the creek roared as it tumbled over the rocks, it was still summer on the porch, warm — even with the sound of raindrops on the glass roof.

I had a playhouse that was the envy of my young friends. It was eight feet square and six feet high, large enough for a small-sized table and chairs where four little girls could have a tea party. On either side of the little front door were two small clear glass windows with tiny vertical inserts of pink roses in art glass. I liked it but was amazed that my little friends made a fuss over it and thought that it was so beautiful. I guess I took it for granted that everyone could have windows with roses in them.

When I had outgrown my playhouse with its art glass windows, I bequeathed it to my brothers. First, it was a club-house, then the "General"-of-the-army headquarters, when the neighborhood scouts drilled in front, and finally, a glorious coop for their project of raising chickens. How many chickens enjoy the luxury of art glass windows to gaze through as they sit upon their eggs? How many little girls peek through the windows of a chicken house and see nests full of real eggs — but Easter-colored eggs made by the reflection of the colored glass windows?

Outside of the playhouse was a tiny lamp with four sides of glass showing the sandman, a little bearded gnome-like creature in red suit carrying a sack of sand over his shoulder. The lamp standard itself was made of bronze in the shape of a European streetlight. I loved that lamp for I thought the little man was the seven dwarfs' brother — the eighth dwarf!

Unbelievable as it may seem, this was not a glass house, but a house of great charm and beauty where the art glass was skillfully used and melded with the architecture.

Is it any wonder that I want to save the few remaining important art glass landmarks of San Francisco? No one can look at these domes, windows and ceilings without enjoying their beauty and perhaps retaining a bit of it.

San Francisco is made up of much that is deeply appealing, whether it be people, scenery, houses, parks or oceans — like art glass every piece is important and cannot be lost.

Mrs. Bert Hopps and the Authors Sister.

EPILOGUE

t may have been William Butler Yeats, who, upon visiting San Francisco, was the first to say (so often repeated) that this city could someday become the Athens of a western Greece.

Sensitive artists were cognizant of the beginnings of artistic activity, and they realized that the destiny of a city is shaped by the architects, musicians, painters and sculptors.

San Francisco, climatically and geographically blessed, with men and women who loved life, could only go in one direction after the devastation of 1906. A rebirth of beauty, inspiration and opportunity was provided by the Panama-Pacific International Exposition in 1915. People from all over the world would visit San Francisco for the first time and this would encourage international trade and cultural exchange.

All of this came to pass; visitors, enchanted with the "Athens of the West", became San Franciscans; the city moved forward in world trade and at the same time progressed in the fields of art and culture. Today, world travelers frequently express their views that San Francisco is one of the world's most fascinating and exciting cities with a distinctive international flavor.

ACKNOWLEDGEMENTS

Mrs. Marilyn P. Larkin
Mr. and Mrs. Donald Falconer
Mr. and Mrs. Terence Ellsworth
Mr. and Mrs. Warren Hanna
Mr. Otto Dressler
Mr. and Mrs. Stuart Adams — Bardelli's
Mr. Martin J. O'Dea — Hibernia Bank
Mr. David Freed — Tobin & Tobin
Mr. Thomas Marquard — Olympic Club
Mr. Charles Sheldon — City of Paris —
Liberty House

Mr. Warner B. Rhoades — City of Paris —
Liberty House

Mr. Franz Munich — Palace Hotel
Mr. James Nassikas — Stanford Court Hotel
Mrs. M. K. Swingle
Messrs. Kutsko Moran Mullin — Victorian House
Cypress Lawn Cemetery Association
California Historical Society
Mr. and Mrs. Valia L. Tellone
Syufy Company

Favorite Subject

Snow White and Dwarfs